Ite
ti
u

Francis Frith's
Gloucester

Photographic Memories

Francis Frith's
Gloucester

Keith Haynes

FRITH
BOOK Co

First published in the United Kingdom in 2001 by
Frith Book Company Ltd

Hardback Edition 2001
ISBN 1-85937-417-4

Paperback Edition 2001
ISBN 1-85937-232-5

British Library Cataloguing in Publication Data

Francis Frith's Around Gloucester
Keith Haynes

Frith Book Company Ltd
Frith's Barn, Teffont,
Salisbury, Wiltshire SP3 5QP
Tel: +44 (0) 1722 716 376
Email: info@francisfrith.co.uk
www.francisfrith.co.uk

Printed and bound in Great Britain

AS WITH ANY HISTORICAL DATABASE THE FRITH ARCHIVE IS CONSTANTLY BEING CORRECTED AND IMPROVED
AND THE PUBLISHERS WOULD WELCOME INFORMATION ON OMISSIONS OR INACCURACIES

Contents

Francis Frith: *Victorian Pioneer*

FRANCIS FRITH, Victorian founder of the world-famous photographic archive, was a complex and multi-talented man. A devout Quaker and a highly successful Victorian businessman, he was both philosophic by nature and pioneering in outlook.

By 1855 Francis Frith had already established a wholesale grocery business in Liverpool, and sold it for the astonishing sum of £200,000, which is the equivalent today of over £15,000,000. Now a multi-millionaire, he was able to indulge his passion for travel. As a child he had pored over travel books written by early explorers, and his fancy and imagination had been stirred by family holidays to the sublime mountain regions of Wales and Scotland. 'What a land of spirit-stirring and enriching scenes and places!' he had written. He was to return to these scenes of grandeur in later years to 'recapture the thousands of vivid and tender memories', but with a different purpose. Now in his thirties, and captivated by the new science of photography, Frith set out on a series of pioneering journeys to the Nile regions that occupied him from 1856 until 1860.

Intrigue and Adventure

He took with him on his travels a specially-designed wicker carriage that acted as both dark-room and sleeping chamber. These far-flung journeys were packed with intrigue and adventure. In his life story, written when he was sixty-three, Frith tells of being held captive by bandits, and of fighting 'an awful midnight battle to the very point of surrender with a deadly pack of hungry, wild dogs'. Sporting flowing Arab costume, Frith arrived at Akaba by camel seventy years before Lawrence, where he encountered 'desert princes and rival sheikhs, blazing with jewel-hilted swords'.

During these extraordinary adventures he was assiduously exploring the desert regions bordering the Nile and patiently recording the antiquities and peoples with his camera. He was the first photographer to venture beyond the sixth cataract. Africa was still the mysterious 'Dark Continent', and Stanley and Livingstone's historic meeting was a decade into the future. The conditions for picture taking confound belief. He laboured for hours in his wicker dark-room in the sweltering heat of the desert, while the volatile chemicals fizzed dangerously in their trays. Often he was forced to work in remote tombs and caves where conditions were cooler. Back in London he exhibited his photographs and was 'rapturously cheered' by members of the Royal Society. His reputation as a

photographer was made overnight. An eminent modern historian has likened their impact on the population of the time to that on our own generation of the first photographs taken on the surface of the moon.

Venture of a Life-Time

Characteristically, Frith quickly spotted the opportunity to create a new business as a specialist publisher of photographs. He lived in an era of immense and sometimes violent change. For the poor in the early part of Victoria's reign work was a drudge and the hours long, and people had precious little free time to enjoy themselves. Most had no transport other than a cart or gig at their disposal, and had not travelled far beyond the boundaries of their own town or village. However,

by the 1870s, the railways had threaded their way across the country, and Bank Holidays and half-day Saturdays had been made obligatory by Act of Parliament. All of a sudden the ordinary working man and his family were able to enjoy days out and see a little more of the world.

With characteristic business acumen, Francis Frith foresaw that these new tourists would enjoy having souvenirs to commemorate their days out. In 1860 he married Mary Ann Rosling and set out with the intention of photographing every city, town and village in Britain. For the next thirty years he travelled the country by train and by pony and trap, producing fine photographs of seaside resorts and beauty spots that were keenly bought by millions of Victorians. These prints were painstakingly pasted into family albums and pored over during the dark nights of winter, rekindling precious memories of summer excursions.

The Rise of Frith & Co

Frith's studio was soon supplying retail shops all over the country. To meet the demand he gathered about him a small team of photographers, and published the work of independent artist-photographers of the calibre of Roger Fenton and Francis Bedford. In order to gain some understanding of the scale of Frith's business one only has to look at the catalogue issued by Frith & Co in 1886: it runs to some 670 pages, listing not only many thousands of views of the British Isles but also many photographs of most European countries, and China, Japan, the USA and Canada — note the sample page shown above from the hand-written *Frith & Co* ledgers detailing pictures taken. By 1890 Frith had created the greatest specialist photographic publishing company in the world,

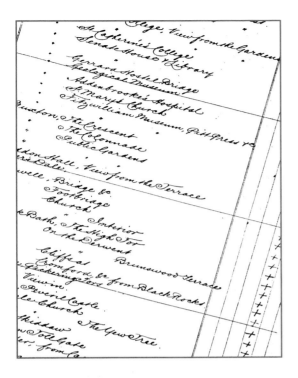

with over 2,000 outlets – more than the combined number that Boots and WH Smith have today! The picture on the right shows the *Frith & Co* display board at Ingleton in the Yorkshire Dales. Beautifully constructed with mahogany frame and gilt inserts, it could display up to a dozen local scenes.

Postcard Bonanza

The ever-popular holiday postcard we know today took many years to develop. In 1870 the Post Office issued the first plain cards, with a pre-printed stamp on one face. In 1894 they allowed other publishers' cards to be sent through the mail with an attached adhesive halfpenny stamp. Demand grew rapidly, and in 1895 a new size of postcard was permitted called the court card, but there was little room for illustration. In 1899, a year after

Frith's death, a new card measuring 5.5 x 3.5 inches became the standard format, but it was not until 1902 that the divided back came into being, with address and message on one face and a full-size illustration on the other. *Frith & Co* were in the vanguard of postcard development, and Frith's sons Eustace and Cyril continued their father's monumental task, expanding the number of views offered to the public and recording more and more places in Britain, as the coasts and countryside were opened up to mass travel.

Francis Frith died in 1898 at his villa in Cannes, his great project still growing. The archive he created continued in business for another seventy years. By 1970 it contained over a third of a million pictures of 7,000 cities, towns and villages. The massive photographic record Frith has left to us stands as a living monument to a special and very remarkable man.

Frith's Archive: *A Unique Legacy*

FRANCIS FRITH'S legacy to us today is of immense significance and value, for the magnificent archive of evocative photographs he created provides a unique record of change in 7,000 cities, towns and villages throughout Britain over a century and more. Frith and his fellow studio photographers revisited locations many times down the years to update their views, compiling for us an enthralling and colourful pageant of British life and character.

We tend to think of Frith's sepia views of Britain as nostalgic, for most of us use them to conjure up memories of places in our own lives with which we have family associations. It often makes us forget that to Francis Frith they were records of daily life as it was actually being lived in the cities, towns and villages of his day. The Victorian age was one of great and often bewildering change for ordinary people, and though the pictures evoke an impression of slower times, life was as busy and hectic as it is today.

We are fortunate that Frith was a photographer of the people, dedicated to recording the minutiae of everyday life. For it is this sheer wealth of visual data, the painstaking chronicle of changes in dress, transport, street layouts, buildings, housing, engineering and landscape that captivates us so much today. His remarkable images offer us a powerful link with the past and with the lives of our ancestors.

Today's Technology

Computers have now made it possible for Frith's many thousands of images to be accessed almost instantly. In the Frith archive today, each photograph is carefully 'digitised' then stored on a CD Rom. Frith archivists can locate a single photograph amongst thousands within seconds. Views can be catalogued and sorted under a variety of categories of place and content to the immediate benefit of researchers.

Inexpensive reference prints can be created for them at the touch of a mouse button, and a wide range of books and other printed materials assembled and published for a wider, more general readership - in the next twelve months over a hundred Frith local history titles will be published! The day-to-day workings of the archive are very different from how they were in Francis Frith's time: imagine the herculean task of sorting through eleven tons of glass negatives as Frith had to do to locate a particular sequence of pictures! Yet

See Frith at www.francisfrith.co.uk

the archive still prides itself on maintaining the same high standards of excellence laid down by Francis Frith, including the painstaking cataloguing and indexing of every view.

It is curious to reflect on how the internet now allows researchers in America and elsewhere greater instant access to the archive than Frith himself ever enjoyed. Many thousands of individual views can be called up on screen within seconds on one of the Frith internet sites, enabling people living continents away to revisit the streets of their ancestral home town, or view places in Britain where they have enjoyed holidays. Many overseas researchers welcome the chance to view special theme selections, such as transport, sports, costume and ancient monuments.

We are certain that Francis Frith would have heartily approved of these modern developments in imaging techniques, for he himself was always working at the very limits of Victorian photographic technology.

The Value of the Archive Today

Because of the benefits brought by the computer, Frith's images are increasingly studied by social historians, by researchers into genealogy and ancestory, by architects, town planners, and by teachers and schoolchildren involved in local history projects.

In addition, the archive offers every one of us an opportunity to examine the places where we and our families have lived and worked down the years. Highly successful in Frith's own era, the archive is now, a century and more on, entering a new phase of popularity.

The Past in Tune with the Future

Historians consider the Francis Frith Collection to be of prime national importance. It is the only archive of its kind remaining in private ownership and has been valued at a million pounds. However, this figure is now rapidly increasing as digital technology enables more and more people around the world to enjoy its benefits.

Francis Frith's archive is now housed in an historic timber barn in the beautiful village of Teffont in Wiltshire. Its founder would not recognize the archive office as it is today. In place of the many thousands of dusty boxes containing glass plate negatives and an all-pervading odour of photographic chemicals, there are now ranks of computer screens. He would be amazed to watch his images travelling round the world at unimaginable speeds through network and internet lines.

The archive's future is both bright and exciting. Francis Frith, with his unshakeable belief in making photographs available to the greatest number of people, would undoubtedly approve of what is being done today with his lifetime's work. His photographs, depicting our shared past, are now bringing pleasure and enlightenment to millions around the world a century and more after his death.

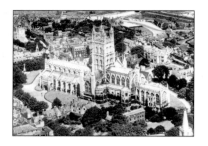

Around Gloucester - *An Introduction*

THE CONTINOUS PROCESS of archaelogy, is still teaching us about the city and its origins, which date back thousands of years. The city of Gloucester stands on the site of an old Roman fortress, and around AD 43, the Christian faith came (literally) floating up the Severn river with the advancing legions from Rome. Here the legions built a Roman station, Glevum, or Gloucester, as we know it today. The site was the first point on the Severn river where a bridge could easily be built; the same reasoning made London such a major centre of residence and business at the time. By AD 97 or thereabouts, it is documented that Gloucester was a self-governing city, or a colonia, as the Romans called it; the title was bestowed on the city by the Emperor Nerva. The famous Roman second legion, which he led, retired

its soldiers and families to the settlement of Glevum from its base in Caerleon (Isca Silurum). Because of this, the area flourished, and became the commercial centre of the Severn Valley. Gloucester enjoyed similar rights to the city of Rome itself. The corners of Brunswick Road and Parliament Street reflect the old defensive land lines of the original fortress, where gateways to the city's core could be found.

In around AD 582, just north of Bath at Deorham (now Dyrham), Ceawlin led his army against Candidianus, a Roman Briton, and two Welsh princes, Fernvael and Cynvael, all of whom represented Britain in Roman terms. All three were killed, and Ceawlin ensured that the whole area, which encompassed Glevum, was passed back in to

English hands. Organised Christian institutions in Glevum perished.

Gloucester formed part of an area called Hwicce after this. King Aethelred of Mercia laid the foundations of a monastery in AD 681. Periods of instability followed: Welsh invasions raked the city, fires through negligence caused damage, and the civil war between Beornwulf (King of Mercia) and Coelwulf, his successor, tore the fabric out of the area and destroyed the foundations laid down by the Romans six hundred years before. Thereafter the Danes encamped about the city and plundered everything, eventually moving on to Mercia. But Alfred the Great moved them on at the battle of Ethandune in AD 878, and passed the city to his daughter Aethelflaed and her husband Aethelred.

In AD 900, Aethelflaed founded a free chapel royal in the city to house the remains of St Oswald, and in 1085 William the Conqueror ordered the Domesday survey from the palace buildings, located in the area that is known as Kingsholm today. Edward the Confessor resided in the city, and so did Alfred the Great himself; Aethelstan, Emperor of all Britain, died in the city in AD 940. After an illness, Rufus, the 'Red King', penned some poetic lines to say that he would never again rule England as a sick man, and Henry I made his son, Robert, Earl of Gloucester.

During the mid 11th century, Ealdred, the Bishop of Worcester, set about rebuilding the monastery buildings in Gloucester. The appointed Abbot was a man called Wulfstan, and in 1072 he was succeeded by Abbot Serlo, the founder of the present cathedral of Gloucester. The real history of the cathedral begins with Serlo, who energetically raised funds for the cathedral buildings; they were to be not only grand, but also sumptuous.

In 1378 a Parliament met in Gloucester that formed the constitutional heritage of the whole of the country. Henry VIII visited the city with Anne Boleyn as his queen, and again with Jane Seymour, after Anne had been beheaded as a traitor. From then on every king and queen would visit Gloucester; Elizabeth I granted Gloucester the privilege of a seaport.

In 1643, during the Civil War, Gloucester was the only supporter of Parliament, whose army of the time had been obliterated. The city stood alone. Colonel Edward Massey, the city's governor, was ready to serve anyone, be it King or Parliament. Prince Rupert had deployed an army of 6,000 cavalry troops on the east of the city, and to the west stood 8,000 infantry. Only some 2,000 men held firm within the city, and it seemed that the city would fall. King Charles I called for Gloucester's surrender and was defied. Meanwhile, Lord Essex amassed an army of 14,000 men from London; defying probability, he marched to save the city - the journey took thirteen days, some say eighteen. The people inside Gloucester's walls were awoken on 5 September by a blaze of cannon fire from Prestbury Hill as Lord Essex announced the arrival

of his troops. The Royalists streamed away from the city walls, and the London army marched in to the city's confines. All Massey had left was three barrels of gunpowder - he had held off the Royalist forces for weeks. Massey was a mercenary soldier, a soldier of fortune, and self-preservation was his motive, but he will always be remembered as the defender of Gloucester.

The monarchy was restored in 1660, and Gloucester has lived a quiet life with little upset since. In 1957 the city was twinned with Trier in Germany, and ten years later with Metz in France. In 1990, Gloucester received major recognition as tourist destination of the year. Little can match the early battles and civil war that Glevum and then Gloucester found itself embroiled in, except of course the discoveries of barbaric crimes in Cromwell Street and Midland Road during the early 1990s. Local resident Frederick West and his wife Rosemary were arrested

for mass murder. The bodies of family members and many others were found buried within their homes.

Today members of the Royal Family own houses in Gloucestershire, and Prince Charles has enjoyed many years of happiness in the area.

The community of Gloucester has flourished, and is now a wide and varied one. Afro-Caribbean and Asian residents live and work in the very centre of Gloucester. Its docks have also flourished since the Second World War, and today stand proudly as a major attraction for tourists and visitors. The city's rugby club have premiership standing, and have carried the professional standard forward as one of the country's leading rugby union clubs. The county cricket club also aspire to remain in the top flight, and are the one-day champions at the turn of the century. And the Tigers of Gloucester City FC are a respected non-league footballing side with a topsy-turvy history.

The Most Famous Cathedral in the World?

Gloucester has many fine buildings, but of course, the main one is its cathedral. It will surprise many people that it has only been a cathedral since 1540. Before that it was only a church, the Benedictine abbey church of St Peter. The history of the building itself will always be uncertain. Indeed, there is some doubt that it was Abbot Serlo who built the Cathedral from its foundations. An earlier bishop, Bishop Ealdred, had furnished Glevum with a church north of the Roman wall of the city; did Serlo totally demolish the church, or did he, as some suspect, alter the structure to form a part of the new church buildings? The answer may lie with the crypt, which boasts work from two different periods and which leads to further speculation. Could it be that Serlo built the main body of the church, and that Bishop Ealdred built the crypt? Or did Serlo add to the crypt? The whole matter is still open to conjecture, which makes the whole structure the more interesting and appealing.

Whatever the case, by the year 1100 the church was dedicated, and notably with the same ground plan as it has today. In 1122 the wooden roof of the central tower burst into flames during a service, and much of the tower was lost. In 1170 the western tower collapsed. How stable was the building? The structure does not have the solidity of Durham or Winchester. However, Helias of Hereford, a man known as a 'building enthusiast' at the time, presided over the rebuilding of the central tower in a very English style, assisted by Abbot Henry Foliot. In 1239 the church was rededicated by Walter Cantelupe, Bishop of Worcester.

Fire again damaged the abbey in 1300. It took seven years to restore it, and Abbot John Thokey took on the challenge of building the new dormitory and the whole of the south aisle of the nave, which was ready to collapse. The windows and vaulting of the aisle stand as witness to his hard work. If there was ever a question over the structure before, there can be none over the restoration work. The cathedral boasts daring and ingenious masonry design; the fact is that the men and women who worked in very dangerous conditions saved the nave from falling down like a pack of cards, or, in the words of Professor Willis, 'like a capsized ship'. Building continued for over two more centuries. King Edward II, killed by his wife's lover Thomas Gurney, was brought to the abbey of Gloucester to lie at rest, and the subsequent great interest in the city brought prosperity to the abbey.

Gloucester is the birthplace of the Perpendicular style. Thokey and his successors all contributed to the Perpendicular nature of the church, and Abbot Wigmore, Abbot Staunton and Abbot Horton can all take the plaudits for continuing the vision of Thokey. The Perpendicular roof vaulting is believed to have been begun by Wigmore and his master builders in about 1350, and the work is unparalleled. The Norman style was superseded, and the ▶

◀ **The Cathedral from the North-East 1891**
28970
This view of the cathedral from the north side shows sheep grazing in what is now almost the city centre.

cathedral's architectural style was not to be seen anywhere else in England. Walter Froucester, a renowned figure in the history of the building, completed the cloisters, which many would say have not been matched anywhere.

The cathedral now had a Norman nave and Gothic vaulting, and a Perpendicular choir and transepts, in a Romanesque outer shell. Morwent would be involved in the south porch in years to come, and Thomas Seabroke planned the cathedral's greatest feature, the central tower. Abbot Hanley and Abbot Farley finished the building off with the Lady Chapel, which left the cathedral as we know it today. The building is not a mis-match of styles and ideas, but rather has been transformed over the centuries by building styles, decoration and refurbishment to leave us with one of the most special buildings that England has to offer.

◄ **General View 1891** 29003
There is no better way to start our visit to Gloucester than by the river, which leads into and by-passes the city quite dramatically. The overwhelming view is always of the cathedral, which splendidly dominates all other structures.

◄ **The Cathedral c1965**
G20101
Surrounding this splendid structure are the houses and local businesses of the city centre that lead to Westgate Street, Eastgate Street, Southgate Street and Northgate Street.

The Cathedral 1892 29899
Another idyllic view of the grand cathedral in the late 19th century. In the background we can see the many hills that surround Gloucester, giving way to all routes north, south, east and west.

The Cathedral from the South 1923 73675
A view of the south porch that Morwent lovingly erected. Note the rich lace-like carving, 'saracenic work'. The porch bonds well with Abbot Thokey's decorated south aisle within.

The Cathedral, the South Porch 1891 28972
Here we see a closer view of the south porch, displaying carved figures of King Osric and Abbot Serlo on either side of the entrance. Across the top of the doorway are the six figures representing St Peter, St Paul and the four evangelists, which were carved by J F Redfern.

The Cathedral, the South Aisle 1891 28989
The south aisle was Abbot Thokey's dream. Imagine a place so beautifully decorated that words cannot describe it.
This view to the south transept is possibly the area where the Perpendicular Gothic style first appeared.

The Cathedral, the Crypt 1891 29000

The crypt contains clear differences in its building style. The original design proved too weak to carry the weight imposed on it. Ealdred was involved in the initial construction, and it is probable that Serlo did the strengthening work. Norman masons' marks are clear to see, but the origins of the crypt are pre-1085, making it one of only five dating from this time in the whole of England.

The Cathedral, the Cloisters 1891 28997

Walter Froucester completed the cloisters after 1381. Abbot Horton had started the work, and John Boyfield carried it on. It is one of the most perfect structures of its kind in existence. Froucester's imagination and dedication, with the expert assistance of Gloucester's finest masons, leaves us in no doubt that this was the summit of his life's work. Imagine the monks as they retired to meditate in this area after dinner until evensong. In the northern gallery is the monks' lavatory, with a gently tapered duct for easy flow.

The Cathedral, the Little Cloisters 1923 73680
During the Protectorate in the 17th century, the cathedral was in danger of being pulled down. The Little Cloister had its roof taken off, and the plants grown in the garden for medicinal purposes and for food were removed. On 9 June 1657, an act was endorsed saving the cathedral and the Little Cloister. The buildings were passed on to the people of Gloucester, and saved.

The Cathedral, the Deanery 1891 29001
The Deanery is located next to the west doorway of the Cathedral, and close by to the extravagant cloisters.

The Cathedral, the East Window and the Reredos 1891 28981
The vast east window is the biggest in England. Believed to have been constructed in 1350 or thereabouts, it was badly damaged during the 17th century when the cathedral's demise was being prepared. In the forefront is the coronation of the Virgin, accompanied by saints and angels. King Osric's memorial is close by, and an oak carving of Robert of Normandy (son of William the Conqueror) can be seen in the centre of the choir. However, Reuben tells us that Robert of Normandy was 'as unstable as water, he could not excel, he was ignoble and hopeless'.

The Cathedral 1923 73677
This view of the cathedral was taken from the Palace Yard, which later became the Close. On this very spot, crowds gathered to witness the execution of Bishop John Hooper in 1555. Hooper was burned at the stake as an example to others. His offence? He was married, and also he did not believe that Jesus was physically present in the Eucharist. 7,000 watchers from the city saw him die and heard him as he shouted 'Lord Jesus have mercy upon me, Lord Jesus receive my spirit'. He took forty-five minutes to burn to death.

The Cathedral, Palace Yard 1891 29002
Here we see Palace Yard as it was before it became the Close. The building on the right is in need of urgent attention, but as we see in photograph 73677, it was maintained very well indeed.

The Hooper Monument 1891 29008
The monument apologises to Bishop Hooper, in a sense. Contemporary reports of Bishop Hooper's execution refer to his tongue sticking out of his mouth after his forty-five minutes of agony, as if he was still trying to speak just one last word. This monument was formerly inaugurated in 1863, and stands at the end of Westgate Street in St Mary's Square.

The Cathedral Approach 1923 73679 This picture shows a shop selling cathedral view postcards next to the SPCK depot and the Diocesan Bookshop, all on the right-hand side of the picture.

The Cathedral from College Street 1950 G20009

College Street was originally only 10ft 9in wide. In the 1890s, the Gloucester Cathedral Approaches Company widened the street for easier access. Gloucester man John Stafford Smith composed 'The Star Spangled Banner', which is why the flag of the USA flies from the cathedral every day. It can be seen from the end of College Street as we enter the cathedral grounds.

St Oswald's Priory 1923 73681

The Priory dates from AD 900. It was founded by Aethelflaed, daughter of Alfred the Great, to house the remains of St Oswald, and it is located in the area now known as Kingsholm. The cathedral looks like a warden keeping an eye over the original free chapel royal.

The Docks of Gloucester

THE PORT OF GLOUCESTER lies near the Bearland courts and the city police station, and has enjoyed a huge resurgence in fortune in recent years. It is the furthest inland port in Great Britain: the Gloucester and Berkeley canal connects the city to the Severn estuary. During the railway expansion of the mid 19th century, masses of produce found its way via these docks, mostly corn, grain and timber; but it would not have been unusual to see convict ships setting off for every corner of the globe, as impressive quays and warehouses sprang up to cater for the new trade.

It was Queen Elizabeth I who granted the city a charter in 1580, which gave it the title of a seaport. For centuries thereafter Gloucester was a major sea artery for trade. In 1654 the very first HMS 'Gloucester' was launched, and in 1982 the tenth was launched. In 1780, over 600 ships were logged as mooring at the dock side.

There are many stirring tales about the docks. For instance, in August 1899, Howard Blackburn sailed his 30ft sloop into Gloucester docks. His starting point had been Gloucester docks in Massachusetts, USA. The sailing took two months, an incredible feat for a man who had lost all his fingers, half of each thumb and most of his toes. It is hard to picture the scene in the docks in the 19th century. We can only imagine the area packed tightly with sailing vessels of all shapes and sizes. Companies such as Haine & Corry, old-established coal and builders' merchants, and Price, Walker & Co in Romans

timber yard, did business here for many years. Later on, war-time submarines would venture into the Severn estuary via these docks and the canal to fight against German aggressors.

Today the docks are well-preserved, and there are plenty of small restaurants, shops and drinking clubs. The City Council is housed in the North Warehouse. The Waterways Museum is a focal point for visitors, with so much to see that it can take a whole day to browse. Many of the vast warehouses remain, now restored, and at every turn there is a reminder of what has gone before. The antiques centre on the dock side, on the site of the old lock warehouse, houses 110 dealers on 5 floors covering 20,000 square feet. Gloucester docks are a visit in themselves. So redolent of the past are these docks that TV film-makers often visit the area, and 'The Onedin Line' was filmed here over a number of years. The Glorious Glosters, a regiment with a long tradition, have their history charted at the Military Museum.

The Docks 1923 73689
Some of these warehouses still preside over the docks today. The Llanthony warehouse is on the right, housing Wait James and Company; similar companies would store salt and grain from all over the world, and even hire out sacks. A London-registered boat is on the left, and Warehouse Number 1 stands beyond that. Ships and nationalities from all over the world sailed and walked these docks for centuries. The barges were often used to store hundreds of tons of timber that overflowed from the quayside.

The Docks 1912 65114

Here we see the Gloucester and Sharpness steam packet office outside Warehouse Number 1 on the left. A pleasure steamer is moored in the foreground; it would take Sunday revellers out on afternoon voyages at the time of this photograph. A pleasure boat builder was located at Westgate Bridge at this time. Note the person working on the packed barge on the right - the distinctive hat could mean that he was a seaman from Asia working from the barge, or maybe he was a lighterman.

Westgate Bridge 1906 55843

This photograph proves that the people of Gloucester enjoyed the waterways of the city in the earlier part of the 20th century. We can see a steam launch and the cabin of a pleasure boat builder on the left of the bridge. The old Foreign bridge used to be close by: here, revenues were collected by St Nicholas church, and later, in 1229, by St Bartholomew's. Locals refer to 'the Island' by the bridge at Westgate. In fact, it has not been an island for many years, but local terminology for places is not easily changed.

The Streets of Gloucester

AS THE FOUR MAIN ROADS, Westgate, Eastgate, Northgate and Southgate Street, meet each other in Gloucester, they form the main focus of the town. Today, the main shopping areas of the city spring from these roads, and to talk of them in separate chapters would be wrong. Over the centuries they have housed a number of well-known citizens of Gloucester, including George Whitefield, the Methodist evangelist, William Ernest Henley, whose prose is read all over the world today, and Charles Wheatstone, who invented the concertina in 1829. Of course there are many more, and we will have a look at many of them in this chapter. But first we must grasp the area as it was, and as it is now. Much has changed, and it should not be lost on us that many inhabitants of the city walk by these buildings every day, with little knowledge of the people they gave birth to and the things they achieved.

The meeting of the four roads is known as The Cross. St Michael's tower, dating back to the 14th century, looks over this point, and the roads lead away from here to the old city gates of Gloucester. Before the tower was built, an old stone cross stood here; however, because of its size and the obstruction of the highway, it was removed. One source tells of its removal in 1754. When we look at the journals of the day, however we read that 'the Antient (the old spelling for ancient) Cross' was removed in the week of 5 November 1751 following an act of Parliament in 1749, decreeing that the streets of Gloucester were to be enlarged, and a number of buildings taken down.

Westgate Street

First we will travel down Westgate Street, and look at the buildings, the people and the times. Westgate Street could boast of being the main road of the four. For years it was the main artery that ran through Gloucester, and linked the towns surrounding the Severn crossing.

As we have already seen, the cathedral stands on the right-hand side of the street as we walk from the crossroads. Westgate once housed the churches of Holy Trinity and St Mary de Grace, which eventually fell into ruin and were removed. A hundred years ago, the King's Board was taken down and rebuilt in Hillfield Gardens. It was a very elaborate Gothic building that was used for the sale of meat and butter, and later used for preaching. Westgate Street, like its sister streets, was packed with thriving businesses, but at the turn of the 19th century it was yet to be the location of businesses like Woolworth's and Boots. They would come later, and nowadays they are located in the Eastgate Street shopping area, which is pedestrianised for safer shopping.

The Old Tolsey, where the affairs of the city were discussed, once stood at the corner of

Westgate Street and Southgate Street; it has since gone. But it would have been a fine sight today, with its wooden carvings leaping out at passers-by. Different trades would gather in the different streets, and Westgate housed butchers and associated meat traders; the cattle market was nearby in Northgate Street. Nowadays Westgate Street unwittingly carries on the tradition - here, we can now find McDonalds and KFC! We can imagine the bustle of this artery route centuries ago. Carts and horses filled the street, carrying cattle and people to destinations that today take only a few hours to get to by car. These journeys could take weeks, and there was also the risk of attacks from criminals who fed off the transport on this route. It was lucky, perhaps, that Gloucester also housed a large correctional institution.

A renowned figure of the time, who was treated as a criminal (of course, he would not be considered one today), was Bishop Hooper; Westgate Street, legend tells us, is the place where he last lodged before his execution at St Mary's Knapp. Beatrix Potter is associated with Westgate Street too. Her famous children's book 'The Tailor of Gloucester' was based on a shop in College Court, close by to Westgate Street as we approach the cathedral. The Duke of Norfolk lodged in Westgate Street when serving his second term as mayor in 1798.

Westgate Street 1923 73666
This view was taken from the cross. Next to Godsell & Sons is Woolworth's, which at the turn of the century was Brinsmead Pianos. If we count four awnings down on the same side of the road, we will just be able to make out Boots. On the left is T Wright, the local tailor, who was first established in the same building in the 19th-century. The street lighting by the chemist was a new innovation, only introduced in 1900 after the generating station opened in Commercial Road.

Westgate Street 1891 29004
Let us compare this picture with 73666 on the previous page. We can see the Theatre Royal below Godsell & Sons, but not in the 1923 photograph. Note the Golden Leg just down from Brinsmead Pianos - what better place to sup some ale after a hard day's graft in Westgate Street. Thirty-four years later, we would find Boots the Chemist (now in Eastgate Street) next door to this establishment.

Westgate Street 1900 45506
The Grate people are still there. On the left a young man stands outside the John Fisher bakery. W H King & Co is closest to us, next to Living Pictures.

Bishop Hooper's Lodging and the Museum 1936 87385

The Crown Inn takes centre stage; it was Bishop Hooper's last resting place before his execution, so it is said. The local council eventually took over the running of these buildings after it became a pharmacy, and resurrected it as a museum.

Western Gate 1892 29908

A young girl looks up at the Western Gate as she poses for the photographer.

The Infirmary Arches 1891 29009
The last two arches are showing signs of some form of reconstruction as the century closes. The Gloucester Royal Hospital now stands away from the city centre, and its architectural style might be described as modern and daunting.

Eastgate Street

IT IS VERY EASY to lose our bearings when we are faced with four such busy streets. If we turn our backs to Westgate Street at the cross, we will face Eastgate Street. Eastgate today is where we find the majority of the bigger stores; leading from it is a shopping arcade on one side, and a market on the other. William Henley was born at number 2 Eastgate Street, and educated at the well-known Crypt School. Eastgate was once called Barton Street; the name still exists today as we walk away from Eastgate towards the new leisure centre site. Eastgate has some tragic stories to tell: a pillory, stocks and whipping post were to be found here, and also over the years fires have been the cause of damage, and indeed loss of life - the fires at the Hippodrome and at Walkers drapery store spring to mind.

The mark of the horseshoe was the mark of Gloucester tradesmen centuries back. It meant that if the work bore the mark of the legendary smiths, it would be famed far and wide. The famous Gloucester Bell foundry stood in Eastgate, and extended to Bell Lane. It was operated by one family, the Rudhalls, for nearly 200 years, and existed for 550 years in total. The wool trade was another great Gloucester tradition, and the docks close by assisted many exports.

Today, the Guildhall houses the new indoor market, and the Beatrix Potter clock is often watched by passers-by as it strikes on the hour. Within this market are found stalls selling all sorts of produce, and also there are a large number of well-known shops, especially clothing shops. But the memories of local people dating back some fifty years will be of Fitch's coffee bar and Rigby's fish stalls. The original market was opened in 1856, but it moved slightly in the 1960s to its current site. Alongside here, on the present Boots building, we can se the beams for the original city gates. Beyond Boots, with our backs still to Westgate, a short walk takes us to smaller shops and Barton Street. Here we are facing Tredworth, and multi-ethnic communities and shops begin to appear as we walk by the leisure centre. Most of what is called Eastgate today used to be Barton Street, which still runs for a long distance away from the city.

Eastgate Street 1892
29906
This scene is virtually unrecognisable to today, but it shows just how busy the four roads of Gloucester were in the 19th century. The delivery men in this picture are prominent. Drinkwater's luggage shop at Number 26 advertises its location on the hoardings. Note the tram lines on the road. All four roads were serviced by trams; in this instance, the line took folk out to the Painswick Road from Eastgate. In 1904 the trams would become electric.

Eastgate Street 1904

51989

A tram approaches the photographer, and a gentleman of the time stands expectantly close to it. It could be that he has just enjoyed a tipple or two in the Saracens Head, which stands alongside him. Or could it be that his local is Fred Ireland's saloon bar, next to the first lamp post on the right?

Eastgate Street 1931
83828
Blinkhorn & Son is clearly to be seen on the left, and beyond that is Currys electrical store, which also sold cycles. The pillars of Eastgate Market announce the entrance to this busy shopping centre. Note the wonderful carvings on the buildings on the right by the old Saracens Head hotel. The cyclist on the extreme right is about to pass the Hippodrome cinema, which burned down in October 1955.

Eastgate Street c1950 G20018
The Saracens Head Hotel is on the right-hand side of the picture as we look towards the Cross. Currys store is still there on the left, and so is Hardy's.

Eastgate Street c1960 G20072
A Gloucestershire Constabulary police officer directs traffic at the cross. He is facing Westgate Street. Dorothy Perkins store is immediately behind him, which today is a genteel coffee shop. Hardy's store is prominent; it was a well-known business retailing furniture. Today this area is pedestrianised, and on the far right is the entrance to Eastgate Market. Banks are now found in Eastgate Street, on the left-hand side of this picture, which eventually leads to the under-cover Kings Walk shops.

Northgate Street

From the Cross, Northgate Street stretches down to the railway station; today it takes about seven minutes to cover on foot. The New Inn could probably claim to be the most historically interesting building in this area. It has certainly been a focal point here for many years. Partially pedestrianised today, Northgate's name is deceiving. It deviates to the east as we progress down the road, and it was the ancient route to Cirencester and London. It was once the site for the main sheep and pig market, whose custodians were often seen chasing the livestock down the street to the amusement of passers-by. Northgate Street now houses the cheaper and larger stores like Wilkinson's and Hyper Value, and a number of shops where you can purchase almost anything vaguely useful for one pound! Jones & Co of Northgate Street could maybe have boasted that they were a superior establishment, for they supplied the decorations and arches that adorned the streets of Gloucester for the visit of King Edward VII in 1909.

Northgate once housed one of the two gaols in the city. Robert Raikes, a local man who pioneered some local reforms in the 18th century, was appalled at the state of these places. Northgate's children suffered hardship and cruelty, and men who could not pay a debt would be housed there until the amount could be paid. How they managed that whilst confined in a cell is questionable. Sundays were troublesome days in the centre of the city, with gangs of children disturbing the quiet. Robert Raikes was effective in bringing peace to the Sabbath day.

But our attention turns to The New Inn. Abbot John Twining built the New Inn in 1455 after the old building at St Peter's Abbey went in to ruin. In the 15th century, Gloucester was a popular and fashionable city, so gentlemen, yeomen, knights and dignitaries were often found within the walls of the New Inn. The chestnut-wood passageway leads inside to rooms that once housed pot rooms and eating areas. Opposite them were stables for horses. Legend states that William Shakespeare once appeared in one of the many plays staged in the courtyard, and as this was the biggest inn in the country, with many dignified persons present, who should doubt it ? As years passed, the advent of coaches and better transport made the inn a port of call for many travelling to London: Northgate remained a trunk route until motorways came to England in the 1950s.

Lady Jane Grey was pronounced Queen of England while she was staying at the New Inn in 1553 - she was only 17 years old. Within months she was charged and sentenced to death by Queen Mary, ultimately the Queen after various challenges to the throne. The first tennis court was built at the New Inn during Tudor times. Like Northgate itself, the New Inn has indeed been a focus for many visitors to the city for hundreds of years. In 1858 the Berry family took over the freehold, which did not change hands until 1942. In 1954 Berni Inns took over the running of the inn, and today the Chapman group run affairs there.

Northgate Street 1936
87381
This photograph was taken from the opposite direction to G20007. We can easily see the New Inn on the left. We can also see that the electric tram lines have now been removed as motor cars take precedence.

◄ Northgate Street
c1950 G20007

This photograph was taken from the cross, the best place to start looking at Northgate Street. Stead & Simpson, the shoe shop, is located four buildings down from the traffic lights on the right. Just down from there we can see the sign for the New Inn. This picture shows a bustling scene at lunchtime.

▼ Northgate Street
Looking towards London
Road c1950 G20019

Here we see the deviation that leads to London, Cheltenham and Cirencester. The TGWU building stands at the junction with Worcester Street. This was known as Coffee House Number Four before the union bought this building. This block also used to house the Theatre Deluxe next to Jays. Opposite Worcester Street was the entrance to the Northgate Wesleyan Chapel. The church spire in the distance is that of St Peter's; it was built between 1860 and 1868, during the pastorate of Canon Calderbank.

◄ Northgate Street 1923 73668

We can see the coffee house at this date. A tram moves towards the cross. The photographer is standing close to Hare Lane, out of shot on the left. Hare Lane was the location for the Old Raven Tavern. Here there was once a plaque stating that this was the brthplace of the Hoare family. They sailed to America in the 'Mayflower', and a member of the family became a member of the legislature of America. It is possible, though, that the actual Ravern Tavern was located in Southgate Street.

Northgate Street 1904
51988
The refreshment rooms on the right advertise their existence by a flag. The photograph shows a bustling and thriving street, with Dolphin Vaults on the left; after the drapery comes Isaac's store, and then Olivers boots and shoes.

◀ **The New Inn 1912**
65118
The courtyard of the New Inn is easily reached from Northgate Street. Legend states that Maria Theresa, the 2ft 10in 'Corsican fairy', was to be seen here in the 18th century, along with a mermaid captured off the coast of Mexico: these shows charged an admittance fee of 6d.

◀ **London Road 1891**
29007
The large flag that overhangs Conway Jones & Co would have been a standard flag for royal visits. Next door is an old fruiterers. The photographer earns much attention from the locals.

▼ **The New Inn c1955** G20048
It is mid-morning in the courtyard of the New Inn. Has the man on the stairway seen the infamous ghost of the New Inn? If we visit here, we too may hear the clattering of hooves in the courtyard around midnight. Or maybe we will receive a visitation from a ghost in a long white robe in the Queen's Suite.

◀ **Kings Square and the Post Office 1936**
87382
As we walk down Northgate Street from the cross, and turn right by Debenhams, we will enter the relatively new area of Kings Square. The Bon Marche in the picture is now Debenhams, and the buildings in the background are in Northgate Street. The square looks out today on a modern townscape of seats and small fountains that leads to Kings Walk and on to Eastgate Street.

Southgate Street

SOUTHGATE STREET LEADS AWAY from the cross towards the docks and the Bristol Road, which today houses a vast number of garages serving the motor trade. The street was created in the 10th century. In 1327 Edward II was murdered. It was decided that he would be buried in Gloucester; legend tells us that his funeral cortège, sparing no expense, made its way into Gloucester via Southgate Street. Large oak beams were held by officers of the law to keep the crowds back as the royal family moved slowly on with the coffin and hearse. After the burial, Gloucester became a place for pilgrims, people who made their way from shrine to shrine, begging and praying.

George Whitefield was born at the Bell Inn in Southgate Street in 1714, and in 1735, attracted by the Oxford Methodists, he stated that he had been reborn as a preacher. His life was one of toil and hard work: he preached over 18,000 sermons in America and in England. He alarmed many people with his preaching - it is recorded that there were convulsions and fainting amongst some of the throngs who looked on. Crowds of 30,000 would gather in some parts of the country, but it is documented that the people of Cheltenham were unresponsive to him. He also ignored a sentence of suspension imposed on him by the church. A chaplain to Lady Huntingdon, he married Elizabeth James in 1741. He continued to raise funds for an orphanage in Georgia (USA); he died in 1770, from 'absolute exhaustion', and

was buried in Newburyport, New Hampshire.

Scriven's conduit was removed from Southgate, near Bell Lane, in 1784. The lead conduit brought water to the city from Robinswood Hill, and was a grand octagonal structure measuring 10ft across. It now stands in Hillfield Gardens.

Robert Raikes was born in Southgate. He was the son of Robert Raikes the Elder, who founded the 'Gloucester Journal', and was educated at Kings School. He was born on 14 September 1735, and he became an enthusiastic Christian. His beliefs led him to set up reading classes at the main gaol, and in time he and Thomas Stock found premises to educate children from the worst homes in the city on Sundays. Fights were frequent in class, and Raikes talks of 'turrible chaps' and 'wild animals'. He encouraged parental responsibility and involvement, and children had to attend with clean hands, clean faces and combed hair. His success influenced all parts of the country, and Queen Charlotte requested his presence at Windsor Castle. His passion for the poor and their education never wavered, and even though he was held up by highwaymen on route to London, he continued his work with the needy. He eventually retired from the 'Journal' in 1802, and worked at the parish church of St Mary de Crypt. In 1811 he died at a ripe old age, and his remains lie at St Mary de Crypt church. It may be argued that Raikes is one of Gloucester's most famous sons.

Southgate Street 1891 29005

On the left we can see Baker's clock, near to their shop; they were well-known clock and watch makers. Two doors down is the Old Blue Shop (which eventually became a tea warehouse) which was painted bright blue. A host of street lamps, which were erected in late 1890, chase their way down the road. The closest is the lamp outside Frederick Wright's County Cigar Store. He supplied the Prince of Wales with Ariston cigarettes. Opposite is the Corn Exchange.

Southgate Street 1904 51987

The Simmonds fleet of buses would often work their way up and down Southgate Street. A typical sight a few years later in 1909 were the steam wagons belonging to the Co-operative society; with their solid tyres they made slow going, but carried immense loads.

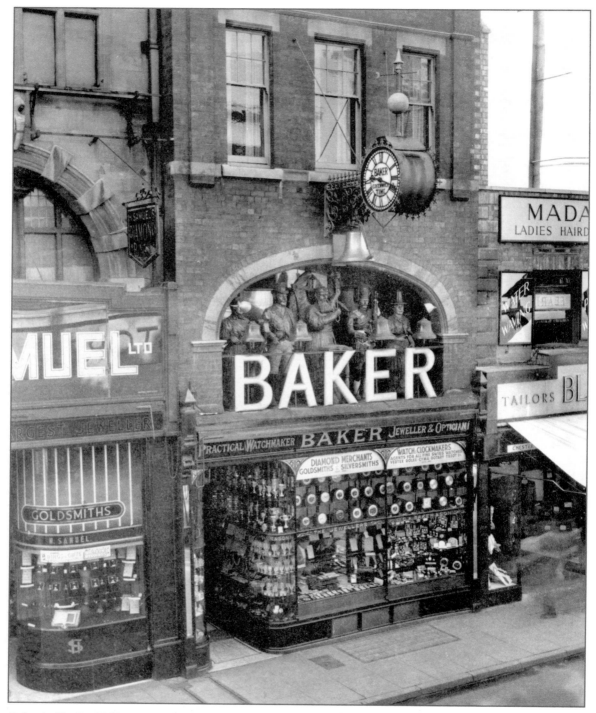

Baker's Clock c1960 G20057
A closer look at the shop and the clock. The national figures installed on the clock did not appear until 1904. An inscription reads: 'Time ball falls daily at 12 o'clock and the barometer under is set at 9am daily'. The five striking jacks represent Wales, Scotland, Ireland, England and, of course, Old Father Time.

Southgate Street 1891 29006
This is Robert Raikes' house, his birthplace. The civilising influence of his Sunday schools on the people of Gloucester was very stabilising.

▼ **Raikes' House 1923** 73686

Note that on the left-hand side at the top of the house the window is missing. Perhaps reconstruction is going on, or maybe repairs are about to start.

▼ **Southgate Street c1950** G20014

Here we have a view looking into Longsmith Street, which leads down to Bearlands police station and the courts. In 1927 Longsmith Street was widened, and vitocrete was laid down as a surface. Longsmith Street leads down to the River Severn and the current prison. In 1906, five convicts made their escape by boat; they were eventually captured.

▲ **Southgate Street c1960**
G20082
The New County Hotel, with RAC and AA signs outside, is prominent in this photograph. This used to be called the Ram Hotel. Again Raikes' house, 38 Southgate Street, stands out.

◄ **Southgate Street c1950**
G20005
The Bell Hotel, now
re-opened, contains a
wonderful old fire surround
for the visitor to see.

**Southgate Street
1923** 73670
Raikes' house looks as
if it may need some
attention at this date.
The awning next to the
house belongs to the
Golden Anchor clothing
company, and on the
other side we can see
Henry Playfair's boot
and shoe shop.

Southgate Street, Raikes' House 1912 65112
The Golden Anchor was still to be found next to Raikes' house in 1912; however, Henry Playfair was yet to take up residence at Number 19.

Southgate Street and Robert Raikes' House c1950 G20004
This view of Raikes' house also shows the New County hotel and grill room. Note the man outside the hotel in trench-coat and hat - a typical fifties outfit.

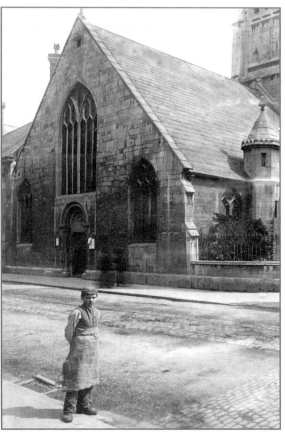

Southgate Street c1955 G20020
The dental repair service stands next to the Stroud Brewery's Berkeley Hunt. Note the cycles outside the building - this was a good stop-off point on the way home from work for workers from the docks and post office.

St Mary de Crypt Church 1891 29010A
The earliest recorded church on this site was the church of the Blessed Mary in 1140. Here stands the tomb of Robert Raikes. Also buried here is the eccentric banking millionaire Jemmy Wood.

**The Sunday School
1892** 29907
Traditionally-dressed
schoolgirls wait outside
the Coach and Horses Inn.

◀ **The Park
the Robert Raikes Statue
1931** 83833
The people of Gloucester
would call Robert Raikes
'Bobby Wildgoose' as he
walked down the road - he
always looked grand. His
pioneering Sunday schools
caught the imagination of
Queen Charlotte, and soon
after Sunday schools
opened in Windsor.

Raikes Sunday School
1923 73687

St Catherine's Knapp, Park Street, is reportedly the site of the first girls' Sunday school, founded by Robert Raikes. Note the boxes in the street and the young boy in front of them - this is Parson's fishmongers, the venue for the filming of 'Pennies from Heaven'.

The Park
the Fountain 1912
65115

A young girl stands to pose in front of the fountains. Christchurch in the background stands in Brunswick Street, which leads, as the crow flies, to Southgate Street. The war memorial now stands in the park too, but of course in 1912 there were two great wars and many conflicts yet to come for the people of Gloucester.

The Park
the Fountain 1900
45516

It seems it is traditional to pose in front of the fountain in the large expanse that is the park. A delivery boy sits between two less interested young men.

The Park 1923 73685

A wonderful view through the park. From here we can visit Spa Road, Brunswick Road and Christchurch. The site of the spa, in Spa Road, was discovered in 1814, and pump rooms were built, but they have now gone. However, the area rivals Cheltenham for its splendid Regency architecture.

The Art Gallery 1912 65116

The art gallery and museum is easily reached from the park. This picture of what was once the Price Memorial Hall in Brunswick Road shows Jennings the printers on the left, with the city steam printing works alongside. The building has been in use as a museum since 1860.

Around the Outskirts

AROUND THE OUTSKIRTS there are a number of interesting sites to view the city from. Many are unexplored by the casual visitor to the city, and indeed by the residents of the city itself. These photographs give lovely views towards the city from various locations, and also hold some interesting features within them.

Lassington Lane 1906 55841
This is the lane at Highnam wood. Today the Lassington mummers perform traditional plays from their Highnam base around the county; they revitalised the custom - the plays were last performed in Gloucester at the start of the 20th century. These plays, centering on the battle between light and darkness, are performed over the Christmas period.

The Lassington Oak 1907 59455
The old oak tree at Lassington is now lying on its side. However, a new tree is now in place and flourishing. The Lassington Oak Morris Men, named after the tree, dance in a fine Cotswold tradition, which brings fine weather, good luck and fertility.

Bentham, The Bridge c1960 B600015
The famed Gloucester composer, John Stafford Smith, lived close by to Bentham at Dog Lane. He composed 'The Star-Spangled Banner'. Today, as we by-pass Gloucester going towards Cirencester, Bentham is conspicuous for the two green domes housing a sports centre, which stand in amongst fields and a small village.

Brockworth, Stroud Road c1955 B837009
The lanes from Bentham lead on to the A46, behind the photographer. Cheltenham is six miles away. This is an early shot of the Crosshands roundabout at Brockworth. The roundabout now houses a large public house and a Shell garage. The old Roman road, Ermin Street, is a right turn off this roundabout. Coopers Hill looms in the distance, the site of the annual cheese-rolling races.

Brockworth, From Castle Hill c1955 B837006
Castle Hill is next to Coopers Hill, and is best accessed from the Abbotswood estate in Brockworth, or from a footpath off the A46. This view shows the village of Brockworth, and what is now the old ICI site and airfield. From here you can not only see the city of Gloucester, but also Cheltenham Spa. On clear days the view takes in the Malvern Hills.

Cranham, The Village 1907 59066
Cranham lies on the other side of Coopers Hill. It is a small village that today is located close to Prinknash Abbey, where monks still live and work.

Painswick, The Cross c1965 P3029
Painswick is easily reached by travelling towards Stroud on the A46 from Brockworth. The winding roads give way to a picturesque village between Gloucester and Stroud.

Painswick, The Church 1900 45597
The church at Painswick has a right-angled, almost fortress-like chapel, which dates back hundreds of years.

Slad Valley 1910 62708
The writer and poet Laurie Lee was born in Slad, and the village and countryside around inspired his most famous book, 'Cider with Rosie'. Upon visiting, one can easily see the reason for such inspirational writing.

Hucclecote, the Village c1965 H337004
As we travel from Brockworth into the city of Gloucester, we come to the suburb of Hucclecote. The village itself goes off to our right and left. Lobleys Drive signals the start of a nature trail, and access can also be found to the ancient hay meadows.

**Barnwood
Barnwood Road c1955**
B529005
Once the site of the old asylum, Barnwood, which comes after Hucclecote, gives access onto Eastern Avenue and the new developments that house commercial DIY stores and electrical businesses.

Barnwood, The Church from the Avenue 1914 66572
This is another view from the same road that passes through Hucclecote to Barnwood, but before the advent of fast cars and lorries. The avenue still remains.

From Robinswood Hill 1904 51985
Robinswood Hill once served the city with water via Scriven's conduit. It is accessed via Reservoir Road, off Eastern Avenue. It now houses the Gloucestershire Wildlife Trust, and affords massive views of the city and, of course, the cathedral.

**Maisemore
The Bridge 1906** 55840
Maisemore village stands
on the west bank of the
River Severn. It is prone to
flooding - in 2000, the
White Hart pub was
completely surrounded
with water. A walk around
Maisemore taking in the
lake is very pleasing.

Over
The Bridge 1906 55842
Over stands close by to
Maisemore on the A40,
encompassing the River
Severn and the River
Leadon. As we pass
Over, one can call in at
the Dog, a pleasant pub.

Longford
Longford Lake 1904
53117
Longford Lake is located close to Sandhurst, and should not be confused with the massive water swells that occur when Plock Court spills over due to rain and bad weather.

**Longford
A Picturesque
Gateway 1904** 53118
Longford is easy to find.
A rest can be taken at
the Longford Inn just off
the A40, and then one
can try to find the
gateway in this picture.

From the River 1923 73673
And finally the river winds its way into the city. The cathedral
stands proud above Gloucester, overseeing the city's affairs,
overseeing the past, and overseeing the future.

Index

Frith Book Co Titles

www.francisfrith.co.uk

The Frith Book Company publishes over 100 new titles each year. A selection of those currently available are listed below. For latest catalogue please contact Frith Book Co.

Town Books 96 pages, approx 100 photos. County and Themed Books 128 pages, approx 150 photos (unless specified). All titles hardback laminated case and jacket except those indicated pb (paperback)

Title	ISBN	Price	Title	ISBN	Price
Amersham, Chesham & Rickmansworth (pb)			Derby (pb)	1-85937-367-4	£9.99
	1-85937-340-2	£9.99	Derbyshire (pb)	1-85937-196-5	£9.99
Ancient Monuments & Stone Circles	1-85937-143-4	£17.99	Devon (pb)	1-85937-297-x	£9.99
Aylesbury (pb)	1-85937-227-9	£9.99	Dorset (pb)	1-85937-269-4	£9.99
Bakewell	1-85937-113-2	£12.99	Dorset Churches	1-85937-172-8	£17.99
Barnstaple (pb)	1-85937-300-3	£9.99	Dorset Coast (pb)	1-85937-299-6	£9.99
Bath (pb)	1-85937419-0	£9.99	Dorset Living Memories	1-85937-210-4	£14.99
Bedford (pb)	1-85937-205-8	£9.99	Down the Severn	1-85937-118-3	£14.99
Berkshire (pb)	1-85937-191-4	£9.99	Down the Thames (pb)	1-85937-278-3	£9.99
Berkshire Churches	1-85937-170-1	£17.99	Down the Trent	1-85937-311-9	£14.99
Blackpool (pb)	1-85937-382-8	£9.99	Dublin (pb)	1-85937-231-7	£9.99
Bognor Regis (pb)	1-85937-431-x	£9.99	East Anglia (pb)	1-85937-265-1	£9.99
Bournemouth	1-85937-067-5	£12.99	East London	1-85937-080-2	£14.99
Bradford (pb)	1-85937-204-x	£9.99	East Sussex	1-85937-130-2	£14.99
Brighton & Hove(pb)	1-85937-192-2	£8.99	Eastbourne	1-85937-061-6	£12.99
Bristol (pb)	1-85937-264-3	£9.99	Edinburgh (pb)	1-85937-193-0	£8.99
British Life A Century Ago (pb)	1-85937-213-9	£9.99	England in the 1880s	1-85937-331-3	£17.99
Buckinghamshire (pb)	1-85937-200-7	£9.99	English Castles (pb)	1-85937-434-4	£9.99
Camberley (pb)	1-85937-222-8	£9.99	English Country Houses	1-85937-161-2	£17.99
Cambridge (pb)	1-85937-422-0	£9.99	Essex (pb)	1-85937-270-8	£9.99
Cambridgeshire (pb)	1-85937-420-4	£9.99	Exeter	1-85937-126-4	£12.99
Canals & Waterways (pb)	1-85937-291-0	£9.99	Exmoor	1-85937-132-9	£14.99
Canterbury Cathedral (pb)	1-85937-179-5	£9.99	Falmouth	1-85937-066-7	£12.99
Cardiff (pb)	1-85937-093-4	£9.99	Folkestone (pb)	1-85937-124-8	£9.99
Carmarthenshire	1-85937-216-3	£14.99	Glasgow (pb)	1-85937-190-6	£9.99
Chelmsford (pb)	1-85937-310-0	£9.99	Gloucestershire	1-85937-102-7	£14.99
Cheltenham (pb)	1-85937-095-0	£9.99	Great Yarmouth (pb)	1-85937-426-3	£9.99
Cheshire (pb)	1-85937-271-6	£9.99	Greater Manchester (pb)	1-85937-266-x	£9.99
Chester	1-85937-090-x	£12.99	Guildford (pb)	1-85937-410-7	£9.99
Chesterfield	1-85937-378-x	£9.99	Hampshire (pb)	1-85937-279-1	£9.99
Chichester (pb)	1-85937-228-7	£9.99	Hampshire Churches (pb)	1-85937-207-4	£9.99
Colchester (pb)	1-85937-188-4	£8.99	Harrogate	1-85937-423-9	£9.99
Cornish Coast	1-85937-163-9	£14.99	Hastings & Bexhill (pb)	1-85937-131-0	£9.99
Cornwall (pb)	1-85937-229-5	£9.99	Heart of Lancashire (pb)	1-85937-197-3	£9.99
Cornwall Living Memories	1-85937-248-1	£14.99	Helston (pb)	1-85937-214-7	£9.99
Cotswolds (pb)	1-85937-230-9	£9.99	Hereford (pb)	1-85937-175-2	£9.99
Cotswolds Living Memories	1-85937-255-4	£14.99	Herefordshire	1-85937-174-4	£14.99
County Durham	1-85937-123-x	£14.99	Hertfordshire (pb)	1-85937-247-3	£9.99
Croydon Living Memories	1-85937-162-0	£9.99	Horsham (pb)	1-85937-432-8	£9.99
Cumbria	1-85937-101-9	£14.99	Humberside	1-85937-215-5	£14.99
Dartmoor	1-85937-145-0	£14.99	Hythe, Romney Marsh & Ashford	1-85937-256-2	£9.99

Available from your local bookshop or from the publisher

Frith Book Co Titles (continued)

Ipswich (pb)	1-85937-424-7	£9.99	St Ives (pb)	1-85937415-8	£9.99
Ireland (pb)	1-85937-181-7	£9.99	Scotland (pb)	1-85937-182-5	£9.99
Isle of Man (pb)	1-85937-268-6	£9.99	Scottish Castles (pb)	1-85937-323-2	£9.99
Isles of Scilly	1-85937-136-1	£14.99	Sevenoaks & Tunbridge	1-85937-057-8	£12.99
Isle of Wight (pb)	1-85937-429-8	£9.99	Sheffield, South Yorks (pb)	1-85937-267-8	£9.99
Isle of Wight Living Memories	1-85937-304-6	£14.99	Shrewsbury (pb)	1-85937-325-9	£9.99
Kent (pb)	1-85937-189-2	£9.99	Shropshire (pb)	1-85937-326-7	£9.99
Kent Living Memories	1-85937-125-6	£14.99	Somerset	1-85937-153-1	£14.99
Lake District (pb)	1-85937-275-9	£9.99	South Devon Coast	1-85937-107-8	£14.99
Lancaster, Morecambe & Heysham (pb)	1-85937-233-3	£9.99	South Devon Living Memories	1-85937-168-x	£14.99
Leeds (pb)	1-85937-202-3	£9.99	South Hams	1-85937-220-1	£14.99
Leicester	1-85937-073-x	£12.99	Southampton (pb)	1-85937-427-1	£9.99
Leicestershire (pb)	1-85937-185-x	£9.99	Southport (pb)	1-85937-425-5	£9.99
Lincolnshire (pb)	1-85937-433-6	£9.99	Staffordshire	1-85937-047-0	£12.99
Liverpool & Merseyside (pb)	1-85937-234-1	£9.99	Stratford upon Avon	1-85937-098-5	£12.99
London (pb)	1-85937-183-3	£9.99	Suffolk (pb)	1-85937-221-x	£9.99
Ludlow (pb)	1-85937-176-0	£9.99	Suffolk Coast	1-85937-259-7	£14.99
Luton (pb)	1-85937-235-x	£9.99	Surrey (pb)	1-85937-240-6	£9.99
Maidstone	1-85937-056-x	£14.99	Sussex (pb)	1-85937-184-1	£9.99
Manchester (pb)	1-85937-198-1	£9.99	Swansea (pb)	1-85937-167-1	£9.99
Middlesex	1-85937-158-2	£14.99	Tees Valley & Cleveland	1-85937-211-2	£14.99
New Forest	1-85937-128-0	£14.99	Thanet (pb)	1-85937-116-7	£9.99
Newark (pb)	1-85937-366-6	£9.99	Tiverton (pb)	1-85937-178-7	£9.99
Newport, Wales (pb)	1-85937-258-9	£9.99	Torbay	1-85937-063-2	£12.99
Newquay (pb)	1-85937-421-2	£9.99	Truro	1-85937-147-7	£12.99
Norfolk (pb)	1-85937-195-7	£9.99	Victorian and Edwardian Cornwall	1-85937-252-x	£14.99
Norfolk Living Memories	1-85937-217-1	£14.99	Victorian & Edwardian Devon	1-85937-253-8	£14.99
Northamptonshire	1-85937-150-7	£14.99	Victorian & Edwardian Kent	1-85937-149-3	£14.99
Northumberland Tyne & Wear (pb)	1-85937-281-3	£9.99	Vic & Ed Maritime Album	1-85937-144-2	£17.99
North Devon Coast	1-85937-146-9	£14.99	Victorian and Edwardian Sussex	1-85937-157-4	£14.99
North Devon Living Memories	1-85937-261-9	£14.99	Victorian & Edwardian Yorkshire	1-85937-154-x	£14.99
North London	1-85937-206-6	£14.99	Victorian Seaside	1-85937-159-0	£17.99
North Wales (pb)	1-85937-298-8	£9.99	Villages of Devon (pb)	1-85937-293-7	£9.99
North Yorkshire (pb)	1-85937-236-8	£9.99	Villages of Kent (pb)	1-85937-294-5	£9.99
Norwich (pb)	1-85937-194-9	£8.99	Villages of Sussex (pb)	1-85937-295-3	£9.99
Nottingham (pb)	1-85937-324-0	£9.99	Warwickshire (pb)	1-85937-203-1	£9.99
Nottinghamshire (pb)	1-85937-187-6	£9.99	Welsh Castles (pb)	1-85937-322-4	£9.99
Oxford (pb)	1-85937-411-5	£9.99	West Midlands (pb)	1-85937-289-9	£9.99
Oxfordshire (pb)	1-85937-430-1	£9.99	West Sussex	1-85937-148-1	£14.99
Peak District (pb)	1-85937-280-5	£9.99	West Yorkshire (pb)	1-85937-201-5	£9.99
Penzance	1-85937-069-1	£12.99	Weymouth (pb)	1-85937-209-0	£9.99
Peterborough (pb)	1-85937-219-8	£9.99	Wiltshire (pb)	1-85937-277-5	£9.99
Piers	1-85937-237-6	£17.99	Wiltshire Churches (pb)	1-85937-171-x	£9.99
Plymouth	1-85937-119-1	£12.99	Wiltshire Living Memories	1-85937-245-7	£14.99
Poole & Sandbanks (pb)	1-85937-251-1	£9.99	Winchester (pb)	1-85937-428-x	£9.99
Preston (pb)	1-85937-212-0	£9.99	Windmills & Watermills	1-85937-242-2	£17.99
Reading (pb)	1-85937-238-4	£9.99	Worcester (pb)	1-85937-165-5	£9.99
Romford (pb)	1-85937-319-4	£9.99	Worcestershire	1-85937-152-3	£14.99
Salisbury (pb)	1-85937-239-2	£9.99	York (pb)	1-85937-199-x	£9.99
Scarborough (pb)	1-85937-379-8	£9.99	Yorkshire (pb)	1-85937-186-8	£9.99
St Albans (pb)	1-85937-341-0	£9.99	Yorkshire Living Memories	1-85937-166-3	£14.99

See Frith books on the internet www.francisfrith.co.uk

FRITH PRODUCTS & SERVICES

Francis Frith would doubtless be pleased to know that the pioneering publishing venture he started in 1860 still continues today. A hundred and forty years later, The Francis Frith Collection continues in the same innovative tradition and is now one of the foremost publishers of vintage photographs in the world. Some of the current activities include:

Interior Decoration

Today Frith's photographs can be seen framed and as giant wall murals in thousands of pubs, restaurants, hotels, banks, retail stores and other public buildings throughout the country. In every case they enhance the unique local atmosphere of the places they depict and provide reminders of gentler days in an increasingly busy and frenetic world.

Product Promotions

Frith products are used by many major companies to promote the sales of their own products or to reinforce their own history and heritage. Frith promotions have been used by Hovis bread, Courage beers, Scots Porage Oats, Colman's mustard, Cadbury's foods, Mellow Birds coffee, Dunhill pipe tobacco, Guinness, and Bulmer's Cider.

Genealogy and Family History

As the interest in family history and roots grows world-wide, more and more people are turning to Frith's photographs of Great Britain for images of the towns, villages and streets where their ancestors lived; and, of course, photographs of the churches and chapels where their ancestors were christened, married and buried are an essential part of every genealogy tree and family album.

Frith Products

All Frith photographs are available Framed or just as Mounted Prints and Posters (size 23 x 16 inches). These may be ordered from the address below. From time to time other products - Address Books, Calendars, Table Mats, etc - are available.

The Internet

Already twenty thousand Frith photographs can be viewed and purchased on the internet through the Frith websites and a myriad of partner sites.

For more detailed information on Frith companies and products, look at these sites:

www.francisfrith.co.uk
www.francisfrith.com
(for North American visitors)

See the complete list of Frith Books at:

www.francisfrith.co.uk

This web site is regularly updated with the latest list of publications from the Frith Book Company. If you wish to buy books relating to another part of the country that your local bookshop does not stock, you may purchase on-line.

For further information, trade, or author enquiries please contact us at the address below:
The Francis Frith Collection, Frith's Barn, Teffont, Salisbury, Wiltshire, England SP3 5QP.
Tel: +44 (0)1722 716 376 Fax: +44 (0)1722 716 881   Email: sales@francisfrith.co.uk

See Frith books on the internet www.francisfrith.co.uk

TO RECEIVE YOUR FREE MOUNTED PRINT

Mounted Print
Overall size 14 x 11 inches

Cut out this Voucher and return it with your remittance for £1.95 to cover postage and handling, to UK addresses. For overseas addresses please include £4.00 post and handling. Choose any photograph included in this book. Your SEPIA print will be A4 in size, and mounted in a cream mount with burgundy rule line, overall size 14 x 11 inches.

Order additional Mounted Prints at HALF PRICE (only £7.49 each*)

If there are further pictures you would like to order, possibly as gifts for friends and family, purchase them at half price (no additional postage and handling required).

Have your Mounted Prints framed*

For an additional £14.95 per print you can have your chosen Mounted Print framed in an elegant polished wood and gilt moulding, overall size 16 x 13 inches (no additional postage and handling required).

---

* IMPORTANT!
These special prices are only available if ordered using the original voucher on this page (no copies permitted) and at the same time as your free Mounted Print, for delivery to the same address

---

Frith Collectors' Guild

From time to time we publish a magazine of news and stories about Frith photographs and further special offers of Frith products. If you would like 12 months FREE membership, please return this form.

Send completed forms to:
The Francis Frith Collection, Frith's Barn, Teffont, Salisbury, Wiltshire SP3 5QP

Voucher for **FREE** and Reduced Price Frith Prints

Picture no.	Page number	Qty	Mounted @ £7.49	Framed + £14.95	Total Cost
		1	**Free of charge***	£	£
			£7.49	£	£
			£7.49	£	£
			£7.49	£	£
			£7.49	£	£
			£7.49	£	£

Please allow 28 days for delivery	*** Post & handling**	**£1.95**
Book Title	**Total Order Cost**	**£**

Please do not photocopy this voucher. Only the original is valid, so please cut it out and return it to us.

I enclose a cheque / postal order for £ . . . .
made payable to 'The Francis Frith Collection'
OR please debit my Mastercard / Visa / Switch / Amex card
(credit cards please on all overseas orders)

Number . . . .

Issue No(Switch only) . . . . .Valid from (Amex/Switch) . . . .

Expires . . . . Signature . . . .

Name Mr/Mrs/Ms . . . .

Address . . . .

. . . .

. . . . Postcode . . . .

Daytime Tel No . . . .   Valid to 31/12/02

The Francis Frith Collectors' Guild
Please enrol me as a member for 12 months free of charge.

Name Mr/Mrs/Ms . . . .

Address . . . .

. . . .

. . . . Postcode . . . .

Would you like to find out more about Francis Frith?

We have recently recruited some entertaining speakers who are happy to visit local groups, clubs and societies to give an illustrated talk documenting Frith's travels and photographs. If you are a member of such a group and are interested in hosting a presentation, we would love to hear from you.

Our speakers bring with them a small selection of our local town and county books, together with sample prints. They are happy to take orders. A small proportion of the order value is donated to the group who have hosted the presentation. The talks are therefore an excellent way of fundraising for small groups and societies.

Can you help us with information about any of the Frith photographs in this book?

We are gradually compiling an historical record for each of the photographs in the Frith archive. It is always fascinating to find out the names of the people shown in the pictures, as well as insights into the shops, buildings and other features depicted.

If you recognize anyone in the photographs in this book, or if you have information not already included in the author's caption, do let us know. We would love to hear from you, and will try to publish it in future books or articles.

Our production team

Frith books are produced by a small dedicated team at offices in the converted Grade II listed 18th-century barn at Teffont near Salisbury, illustrated above. Most have worked with the Frith Collection for many years. All have in common one quality: they have a passion for the Frith Collection. The team is constantly expanding, but currently includes:

Jason Buck, John Buck, Douglas Burns, Heather Crisp, Isobel Hall, Rob Hames, Hazel Heaton, Peter Horne, James Kinnear, Tina Leary, Hannah Marsh, Eliza Sackett, Terence Sackett, Sandra Sanger, Shelley Tolcher, Susanna Walker, Clive Wathen and Jenny Wathen.

Free Print - see overleaf